DISCARD

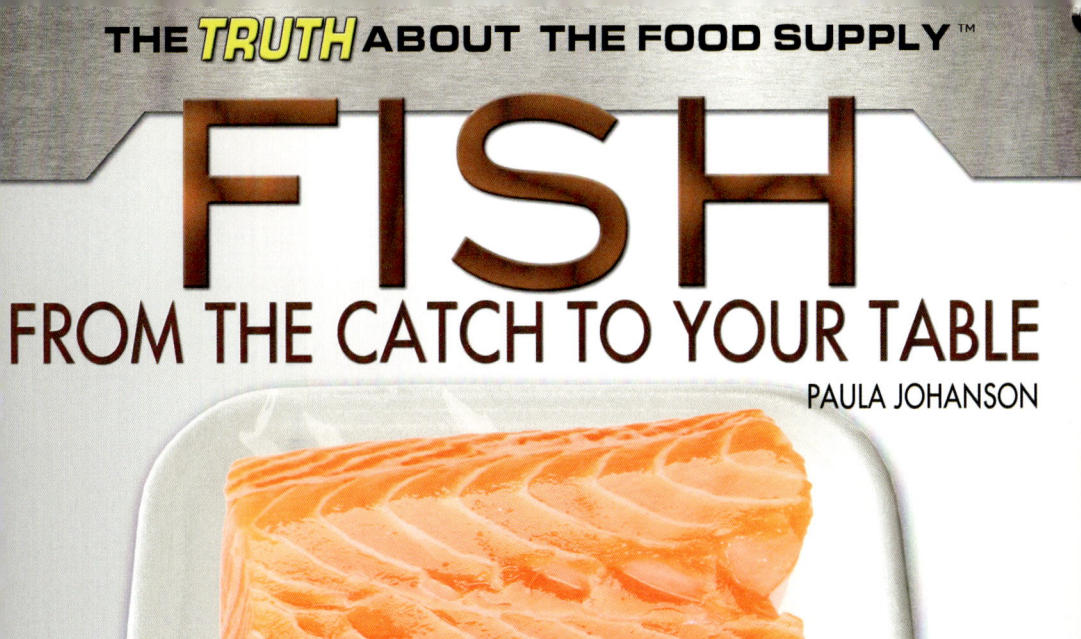

THE TRUTH ABOUT THE FOOD SUPPLY™

FISH
FROM THE CATCH TO YOUR TABLE

PAULA JOHANSON

rosen publishing's
rosen central®
New York

For the Department of Fisheries and Oceans, which had no answers for my uncle when he found a blob of mercury inside a fish he had just caught. And once again, for the salmon run in Goldstream River.

Published in 2013 by The Rosen Publishing Group, Inc.
29 East 21st Street, New York, NY 10010

Copyright © 2013 by The Rosen Publishing Group, Inc.

First Edition

All rights reserved. No part of this book may be reproduced in any form without permission in writing from the publisher, except by a reviewer.

Library of Congress Cataloging-in-Publication Data

Johanson, Paula.
 Fish: from the catch to your table/Paula Johanson.—1st ed.
  p. cm.—(The truth about the food supply)
Includes bibliographical references and index.
ISBN 978-1-4488-6801-8
1. Fish as food—Juvenile literature. 2. Fisheries—Juvenile literature. 3. quaculture—Juvenile literature. I. Title.
TX385.J64 2013
338.3'727—dc23

                                        2011046367

Manufactured in the United States of America

CPSIA Compliance Information: Batch #S12YA: For further information, contact Rosen Publishing, New York, New York, at 1-800-237-9932.

CONTENTS

INTRODUCTION
4

CHAPTER 1
WHAT'S THE CATCH?
7

CHAPTER 2
BEING PREPARED
13

CHAPTER 3
ON THE ROAD
22

CHAPTER 4
IN THE NETWORK
28

CHAPTER 5
MAKING THE RULES COUNT
35

GLOSSARY
41

FOR MORE INFORMATION
43

FOR FURTHER READING
45

BIBLIOGRAPHY
46

INDEX
47

INTRODUCTION

It's a cliché to say there are plenty of fish in the sea. In some places, the abundance of fish really shows. When explorer John Cabot came to Newfoundland in 1497, there were uncountable schools of cod on the Grand Banks, miles offshore. Baskets lowered from ships were pulled up full of fish.

For thousands of years, American Indians caught cod with lines and nets from small boats close to shore. For 450 years after Cabot's arrival, people crossed the Atlantic Ocean to harvest cod on the Grand Banks. There was always plenty of cod to catch in nets that two or three fishermen would pull onto their boat. Some cod were

The hard work of fishing can be challenging but very satisfying. Some people work for a lifetime on the boats and docks, while some work for just one season.

eaten fresh, but most were dried with or without salt. Each year, many thousands of tons of dried cod were shipped throughout Europe and later to the Caribbean and North America. Cod was a reliable part of the international food supply.

After World War II (1939–1945), the technology of fishing changed. Larger nets were used—huge purse seines and beam trawls. These nets went deeper than those used earlier. Powered winches pulled loads to the surface and onto fishing boat decks. Harvesting increased dramatically in the 1950s. Boats came from all over the world to the Grand Banks.

Not only were young and adult cod being caught, the bigger mature cod were also being taken. These "mother fish," as the old fishermen told young deckhands, did most of the breeding.

FISH
FROM THE CATCH TO YOUR TABLE

Without these successful breeders laying thousands of eggs, there were few eggs laid by the smaller females. Habitat for young cod to hatch and grow was battered and destroyed by beam trawlers that dragged chains.

In twenty years, fishing fleets had to look with sonar scanners to find any schools of cod. By the 1990s, there were no schools to be harvested. Canada's government and the United Nations had to put a ban on cod fishing on the Grand Banks. Samples taken by marine scientists show that there are only a few thousand small cod left. Commercial harvesting of cod in this region is not expected to be possible ever again.

The cod resource on the Grand Banks was destroyed not by any one person, but by many fishermen. In many countries around the world, people are learning that lesson so that it won't happen again. People do make mistakes about harvesting fish or processing it for market. Many mistakes are honest errors by people trying hard to earn a living by supplying good food to customers. The more scientists learn about seafood and oceans, the better people can understand their food supply.

"We'll need to farm the seas to survive in a crowded world," Bryan Walsh, who writes about environmental issues, noted in *Time* magazine. "But the challenge will be to do it right." Food regulations control how food is processed and marketed. Environmental and industrial regulations can help manage seafood resources. When citizens participate in making and enforcing good regulations, the food supply is safer and more secure.

Chapter 1
What's the Catch?

In the science of fisheries, "fish" means aquatic animals harvested by people. That includes bony fish and cartilaginous fish like sharks and rays. Fisheries science even includes invertebrates such as shrimp, crabs, lobsters, oysters, clams, squid, octopuses, sea urchins, sea cucumbers, and jellyfish. For seafood, people also harvest seaweed. Traditionally, marine mammals such as seals and whales were killed for meat and oil.

The U.S. Fish and Wildlife Service, a bureau within the U.S. Department of the Interior, works to protect and enrich fish, wildlife, and plants and their habitats for the benefit of the American public. The bureau's Fisheries and Habitat Conservation program helps manage fish species and conserve their natural environment. It works with state agencies, landowners, industries, and other federal agencies to protect fish.

Fish on the Line!

People have caught fish by hand since before humans invented fishhooks and nets. Some anthropologists have

FISH
FROM THE CATCH TO YOUR TABLE

theories that seafood was an important part of the diet for early humans. There are carvings four thousand years old in the Great Pyramid at Giza showing people catching fish with handheld nets.

On a modern fishing boat, fishermen learn to handle hard work and bad smells. One deckhand spoke of killing seven hundred or

Traditional fishermen are family members and friends working together, like this grandfather and grandson fishing with a gill net near Massachusetts.

WHAT'S THE CATCH?

eight hundred fish every day. He and the other deckhands would go ten days without changing their pants. By the time the freezer hold was full, their clothes were stiff with blood and fish slime.

Nearly 8 billion pounds (almost 4 billion kilograms) of seafood was caught in the United States, bringing in about $4 billion in 2009, according the National Marine Fisheries Service.

The work is dangerous. "Fishing is the deadliest job in the U.S.," according to an article in *Time* magazine. The Centers for Disease Control and Prevention noted on its Web site that the U.S. Department of Labor's Bureau of Labor Statistics reported, "During 1992–2008, an annual average of 58 deaths occurred (128 deaths per 100,000 workers), compared with an average of 5,894 deaths (4 per 100,000 workers) among all U.S. workers."

Modern Technology

Fishermen watch currents, seabirds, and seals to find fish. "In times of peace, technology developed in the interests of national security—radar, echo-location, and the like—is constructively redeployed within the fishing fleet," said BBC journalist Nick Fisher. "Engines got faster; fuel got cheaper (and subsidized); weather forecasting became increasingly accurate." New boats traveled farther and for longer than ever before. They also fished much deeper, to depths of about 1,000 yards (914 meters) with huge purse seines. Helicopter pilots now look for tuna schools in particular and radio their GPS position to fast boats.

FISH
FROM THE CATCH TO YOUR TABLE

Floats hold up this purse seine net. The bottom is gathered by a motor on the fishing boat, making the net into a huge bag or purse.

Damaged Ecosystems

Beam trawling scares fish up from the sea bottom. "Over the last decade, the number of deep-sea, bottom-trawl tows off our coast has increased tenfold," wrote marine conservationist Scott Wallace. "These trawls damage large tracts of deep-sea benthic ecosystems…These systems have taken millennia to develop but only decades to unravel." An iron beam about 32 feet (10 m) in length is lowered by a fishing boat. The beam drags heavy chains along the soft seabed, driving fish up into a large net trawled behind the beam. The sea floor habitat is smashed.

"Greenpeace has long been calling for a total ban on beam trawling, which it sees as a threat to one of the planet's last great strongholds of biodiversity," wrote British TV personality and journalist Hugh Fearnley-Whittingstall. "Its Web site invites us to 'think of it as driving a huge bulldozer through an unexplored, lush and richly populated forest—and being left with a flat, featureless desert.'"

Fish Farming

Given the risks of fishing at sea, and the reduction of fish in rivers that run past towns and farms, it's not surprising that fish farms were developed. Fish farms have been common for thousands of years in China. There, most farmed fish are carp or tilapia—breeds that thrive in freshwater ponds and containers.

"We now get about half our seafood from farms," observed editor Richard Stengel of *Time*, including shrimp and other shellfish. "Aquaculture may be the way to save the oceans and its stocks of wild fish and keep everyone fed (and healthy), but there are downsides, too." It takes about 2 pounds (about 1 kg) of wild fish ground into feed pellets to raise about 1 pound (about 0.5 kg) of farmed fish. Another downside is the introduction or escape of foreign fish, such as Asian carp in the Illinois River, which empties into Lake Michigan. These fish become invasive species crowding natural habitat.

Salmon farms raise salmon in large containers for the first year or more. Then for two or three years, salmon are raised in large ocean nets with floating docks. "In the last two decades, global consumption of salmon has risen from 27,000 tons [24,494 metric tons] to more than 1 million tons [907,185 metric tons] annually," wrote journalist McKay Jenkins. Most of that increase

FISH
FROM THE CATCH TO YOUR TABLE

Bycatch

When a net's catch is dumped on a boat's deck, it includes sea animals that weren't wanted. Industry calls these "trash fish" and throws them away. Many kinds of fish can't survive being hauled to the surface. This bycatch of dead and dying fish feeds seagulls, or it rots and sinks.

Bycatch includes sea mammals, turtles, and birds, as well as invertebrates and fish. Lost and abandoned nets drift through the ocean for years without decaying, still trapping and killing fish and animals. "The annual level of discards has been estimated to be some 27 million tonnes [29.7 million tons]," reported marine biologist Daniel Pauly, "a staggering figure in the context of a total world catch of less than 100 million tonnes [110.2 million tons]."

is farmed fish. "The rapid growth of aquaculture has been accompanied by environmental costs," Bryan Walsh wrote for *Time*, adding that "salmon farms… helped spread disease among wild fish while releasing waste into coastal waters."

Shellfish Harvesting

It's fun to dig for clams in beach sand and gravel. This work is so casual, it wasn't until 2006 that traditional clam harvesting was recognized by anthropologists as aquaculture. From Alaska to California, American Indians built clam gardens and tended them for thousands of years.

Most of the oysters and mussels sold in the United States come from shellfish farms. Large nets and docks protect areas where shellfish are growing in mesh bags and on frames.

CHAPTER 2

Being Prepared

In many places around the world, freshly caught fish is eaten right away. The internal organs and gills are removed, and the scales are scraped off. The fish is washed to remove blood and slime.

When a person catches fish for dinner, a small whole fish or a fillet of meat goes into a frying pan or baking dish. Fish heads, fins, tails, and backbones often end up simmered in a pot to make broth before scraps are given to pets or composted.

Industrial, or commercial, fishing cleans fish onboard ships or in a nearby shore-based plant. A Hazard Analysis Critical Control Point (HACCP) system, the U.S. Food and Drug Administration's rules for the food processing industry, ensures that food safety is being considered whenever fish is being processed or prepared. The fish is washed, sorted, inspected, and graded. Scraps are usually discarded at sea as waste. Worldwide, hundreds of tons of fish offal (internal organs) are dumped off boats, along with bycatch.

Some shore-based processors collect by-products from processing fish. Offal can be pressed to remove fish oil. Both the oil

FISH
FROM THE CATCH TO YOUR TABLE

Small boats allow people to fish close to shore, in a variety of habitats. Some fishermen follow seabirds to find schools of fish, and seagulls follow the boats for scraps.

and ground-up offal are used in animal feed and fertilizer and industrially in paints, coatings, and cosmetics.

Preservation Methods

Seafood is 75 percent to 80 percent water. Slowing water activity in fish flesh slows chemical reactions that break down flesh. Because the flesh of fish has less collagen than land animals, fish will spoil quickly. That's why fish is kept cool, or preserved until it is eaten. One or two days after it has been caught, a fish may already be too rotten for a person to eat without getting sick.

People have learned many ways to preserve fish. Heating or irradiation kills germs. Freezing slows spoilage. The processes of smoking, salting, or drying control water activity. In Scandinavia, fish is fermented. Each treatment affects the taste, texture, and nutrition of the fish product.

BEING PREPARED

Canning

During the Napoleonic Wars (1800–1815), canning was invented for soldiers to carry preserved, cooked food. Lead seals and metal cans leached into food until manufacturers learned to make enamel linings. Today when boats come to a cannery, the holds are emptied onto conveyer belts that bring fish to workers. In minutes, each fish is butchered and cleaned, then sliced into cans, sealed, and cooked. Workers must be careful not to be injured doing this tiring work. Some modern canneries use automatic machinery.

Most fish canneries are in Asia and Europe. The Stinson Seafood Plant was the last sardine cannery operating in Maine—and the United States—when it closed in 2010.

Dried Fish

Drying is the world's oldest-known food preservation method. Dried fish can be stored for several years. The product is easy to transport. Cod dried with salt is called salt cod. Fish dried without added salt is called stockfish. For cod without salt, it takes longer for the fish to dry, but processors don't have to buy or make salt.

FISH
FROM THE CATCH TO YOUR TABLE

Frames suspend fish in midair. Usually, fish are cleaned and split through the back with their spines removed, but the tail remains to hold both sides together. It can take weeks for fish to dry thoroughly. Modern solar dryers produce dried fish products in days, and they protect against insects or rainstorms.

Fish Eggs

A traditional treat still enjoyed today is fish eggs, or roe. Sturgeon eggs from the Black Sea are canned and sold as caviar. Japanese sushi includes eggs of salmon, smelt, flying fish, or herring, as well as sea urchins. In North America, a small harvest of herring spawn caught on seaweed is served fresh or smoked in very exclusive sushi restaurants.

People with allergies need to read the ingredients label before buying frozen fish sticks. The breading has wheat flour. Corn and soy flours are often added, as well as salt.

Frozen Fish

In 1920, U.S. government field naturalist Clarence Birdseye watched Inuit guides supply his camp for a journey, catching fish through holes in sea ice. Fish froze solid in minutes after being placed on top of the ice. Days later, the Inuit guides thawed the frozen fish, and it tasted

BEING PREPARED

fresh. Birdseye invented methods to quick-freeze fish, meat, and vegetables. Fish fillets cut in slim blocks froze very well. Coating slices of fish in breadcrumbs made "fish sticks" even easier to cook.

Cooling fresh-caught fish for transport requires at least as much ice as there is fish in a hold. Many fish are quick-frozen within minutes of being caught to kill parasites. Slow-freezing forms large ice crystals in the flesh. On thawing, ruptured cells leak water and flavor. The result is fish that is dry and tasteless. But if fish is frozen within one hour, the ice crystals that form are small and cause minimal damage to the cells. Most "fresh" fish sold in supermarkets or fish markets in North America is thawed after this deep-freezing method.

Smoked Fish

Fish is smoked in forced-air smokehouses with smoke from wood or sawdust. The fish is soaked first in a brine solution of salt and spices, then it is dried on racks in the smoke. In the cold-smoking method, fish is not cooked and keeps well in a refrigerator for months. More commonly, fish is hot-smoked so that it is cooked, too, but it keeps for only a few days in a refrigerator.

Vacuum Packing

One of the ways to keep fish from going bad is to wash it, then seal it in plastic wrap. Air is sucked out of the package, making it vacuum-packed. Fish can be kept cold in a fish market without being contaminated by germs from hands or the air. If frozen, the fish will

FISH
FROM THE CATCH TO YOUR TABLE

Vacuum-packed fish doesn't leak fishy juices on the way home. But the chemicals that make the plastic food wrap flexible can soak into the food. These chemicals affect human health.

not get a "freezer-burned taste" by losing moisture and taste to air inside the package. Unfortunately, bisphenol A and other chemicals in plastic wrap can soak into vacuum-packed food.

Irradiated Seafood

Fish products can be pasteurized or sterilized of germs by using a controlled amount of radiation from an electron beam generator or radioactive elements. This irradiation process is accepted by only some members of the food industry. Not everyone feels confident about using radiation on food because eating only irradiated food has not been proven to be safe in the long term.

Since the 1950s, scientists have studied the irradiation of seafood. The shelf life of fresh fish may be extended up to several

BEING PREPARED

weeks by using low-level doses of ionizing radiation to kill micro-organisms. The taste and texture are not affected. Radiation causes vitamin and enzyme loss in the food, so it is harder to digest and some nutrition is lost.

Fish Products

Many processed fish products are shaped out of scraps of white fish such as pollock, carp, or mullet. Fishcakes are breaded and

Is this crabmeat? No, it's pollack, stained with red dye. Crab juice or artificial crab flavor is added, along with enzymes or egg whites to glue the cooked fish together.

easy to microwave. Imitation, or fake, crab has crab juices and a little red food dye added. Gefilte fish is minced fish stuffed into fish skin and poached. The Japanese make a gelled fish product called *surimi*. These factory-processed foods have chemical additives to keep flesh firm and oils from going rancid. One additive, MSG, causes asthma attacks and headaches, including migraines, in some people. Other additives in processed foods have effects that add up over time to cause neurological problems.

On the Half-Shell

Algal blooms called red tides cause temporary closures of shellfish harvesting areas along seacoasts. When algae build up in shellfish, they cause toxins such as paralytic shellfish poisoning (PSP). The clams, mussels, and oysters survive, but they are poisonous to humans, even after they are cooked.

Oysters from the Gulf of Mexico are contaminated in summer months by *Vibrio* bacteria. Of the thirty or more people infected by these bacteria each year, half will die. Since 2003, the state of California imports oysters only after postharvest processing has been done. The processes of quick-freezing, frozen storage, high pressure, mild heat, or low-dose irradiation kill *Vibrio* and other bacteria. In California, oyster-related deaths are now zero. In states that do not require processing, *Vibrio* infections and deaths continue to occur.

BEING PREPARED

MYTHS AND FACTS

Myth: There are plenty of fish in the sea.
Fact: There aren't plenty of fish in the sea anymore, particularly not the big fish like tuna and salmon. Huge nets take every fish in an area, leaving few to reproduce. Dragnets destroy habitat, so few young fish survive.

Myth: No one knows where the fish on our tables come from.
Fact: Any reputable fish market, restaurant, or fisherman can tell where the fish were caught. Read labels on packaging. The Monterey Bay Aquarium Seafood Watch has online resources to show consumers what questions to ask (http://www.montereybayaquarium.org/cr/seafoodwatch.aspx).

Myth: The ocean is so big, it rids itself of pollution.
Fact: Pollution from garbage and sewage gathers along shores and near cities. Germs, plastics, and heavy metals are in seafood.

CHAPTER 3

ON THE ROAD

Seafood is transported, marketed, processed, and labeled, often thousands of miles away from where it is harvested. "A century ago…the food supply depended on local production and was largely decentralized," observed author Marion Nestle, Paulette Goddard Professor of Nutrition, Food Studies, and Public Health and professor of sociology at New York University. "Fish, for example, were caught wild from the sea." But now, 95 percent of the farmed seafood Americans eat is farmed overseas.

Many people who enjoy Chilean sea bass fillets or canned tuna from Southeast Asia have never eaten a local fish. "Eighty-four percent of seafood consumed in the United States is now imported," reported journalist Elizabeth Rosenthal, "often passing through a multistep global supply chain." Transporting seafood great distances uses more resources than harvesting it.

LOCAL FOOD INCLUDES LOCAL FISH

The 100-mile diet suggests that people try to return to the tradition of eating food harvested within 100 miles (161 km) of where

ON THE ROAD

they live. Another alternative to modern processed food being transported hundreds of miles is the Slow Food movement, which encourages traditional cooking and sustainable harvesting. Both of these movements encourage people to enjoy locally harvested crops and seafood, saving money and resources on transporting food. It's not just for small businesses. Even the international restaurant chain McDonald's serves some regionally harvested seafood. Since the late 1990s, the McLobster sandwich has been available only in the New England states and Canada's Atlantic provinces. "It's a canny move for a quick-serve restaurant that,

Lobster can be a luxury or a simple standard food. When families are looking for fast food, or local treats, seafood can be a good, healthy choice.

um, doesn't often embrace the local food movement," commented a *Globe and Mail* reporter in 2011. There was also a McCrab sandwich, similar to a Chesapeake crab cake, marketed in Delaware, Maryland, and Virginia. The example of McDonald's shows that restaurants of any size can serve at least some local seafood.

Packaging

Many people around the world use wicker baskets and jute bags to transport fish. Straw mats are tied around bundles of dried fish. Fish oil used to be kept in pottery jars, but now it is usually stored in enamel-lined cans. Packaging is reused many times, lasting up to five years. Fish processors must be careful about cleanliness. Washing used packaging and drying it in sunshine kills many germs that can make people ill.

For processed food, chemical plasticizers such as bisphenol A are used in a variety of food containers, including plastic wrap on vacuum-packed fish. Bisphenol A is also in the enamel linings of some cans. But labels on food packages don't mention this toxic chemical that has been linked to fertility problems and cancer. "Should food containers be required to tell consumers not only what is in the food but what goes into the containers themselves?" asked McKay Jenkins.

When food packaging gets thrown away, trash can pile up along seashores or in the ocean when garbage barges are dumped. "In November 2010, BC [British Columbia], Oregon, Washington, and California committed to new initiatives to address man-made marine debris," according to the United Nations Environment

ON THE ROAD

Programme, "including collaborative action on packaging-product stewardship." New laws are being written so that packaging makers will be responsible for the trash from their products.

Read Labels

Labels list ingredients in processed seafood (in descending order of amount), place of the manufacturer, weight, a "use by" or "best before" date, and basic nutrition facts (including number of calories, protein, carbohydrates, fat, and sodium). According to current U.S. law, nutritional information is required only if the product is making a nutritional claim (for example, it is low fat). Labels sometimes include harvesting and processing methods. Since 2005, the seafood market has seen a wide range of new ecological labels and certification programs through the U.S. Food and Drug Administration (FDA) and international agencies. These labels and programs help consumers and businesses identify products supporting environmental and sustainable goals. Legislation protects consumer safety and responds to citizen concerns. In the European Union, food labeling is regulated even more strictly and precisely than in the United States and Canada.

When the FDA discovers that fish products have been mislabeled, it has the power to send warning letters to companies that are in violation of rules, seize seafood products, or prevent the companies

What's in a can? The lining lets chemicals soak into the food. Medical studies are being done to determine the chemicals' effects on human health.

FISH
FROM THE CATCH TO YOUR TABLE

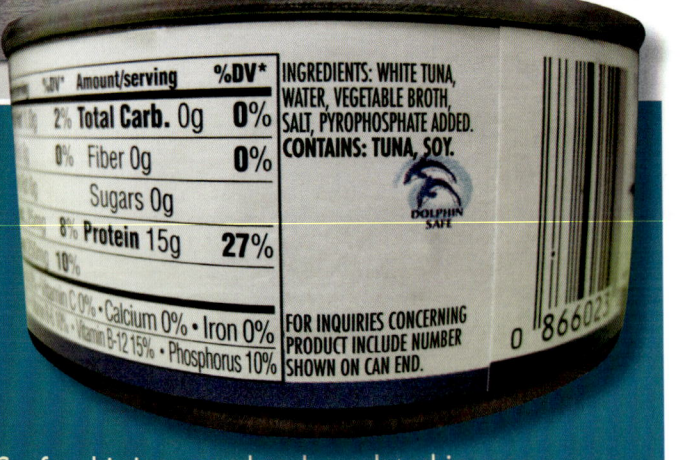

Seafood is inspected and regulated in many countries. The inspectors are concerned with food safety and accurate labeling. Government legislation sets standards for the fishing industry.

from importing fish. However, FDA officials declare that it is mainly the responsibility of states and local agencies to regulate retail food stores and restaurants, according to the article "Mystery Fish," published in *Consumer Reports*. The article also noted that FDA inspectors are not trained to distinguish the different fish species. Their priority is on food safety because of the department's limited funds.

The National Marine Fisheries Service, within the U.S. Commerce Department, and Customs and Border Protection, within the Department of Homeland Security, help the FDA detect and prevent seafood species fraud. These agencies have laboratories that test fish to spot whether the seafood listed on the label is what is really in the package.

RENEWABLE RESOURCE

When fish stocks are first harvested commercially, the largest fish are caught. The resource seems huge. But the first harvests are much larger than a sustainable harvest for long-term production.

Fish are not mineral resources to be mined only once. They are part of an ecology that, if managed well, can be a lasting

ON THE ROAD

food supply. "Without aquaculture, the pressure to overfish the oceans would be even greater," wrote Bryan Walsh in *Time*. "You're not feeding the world sustainably if you need to remove the base of the marine food chain to do it."

The Food Web

Awareness of the food web encourages people to make good food choices and insist on sustainable harvesting methods. "Overfishing punches holes in oceanic webs of life," wrote an editor for *Wired Science*. A coalition of ocean activists and scientists presented their findings to the United Nations. They advised nations to strengthen the protections offered to major ocean fisheries, particularly in international waters. Their report was summed up by Nathaniel Groneword in *Scientific American*, saying the world's oceans appear to be heading toward a new mass extinction event.

Agricultural Commodity

More herring were being fed to animals and used as fertilizer in the 1960s than were eaten by humans. Between 1950 and the mid-1960s, the number of herring worldwide dropped by half. Since 1990, the herring fishery in the North Sea has shown a slow but encouraging recovery. "More than the decimated cod, the herring has shown signs that it may be capable of coming back from the brink [of extinction]," wrote BBC journalist Fisher. "If it does, we can't take much credit. But we can endeavor not to make the same mistake twice." A third of the herring harvest is still being fed to livestock.

CHAPTER 4

IN THE NETWORK

Fish is food that has to be handled much more carefully than vegetables or the meat of land animals. After a day sitting in hot sunshine, a carrot is still food. But a fish will smell bad and become rotten. Fish must be kept cold after it is caught and eaten within two days or frozen. It's best to buy fish or shellfish from a reputable fish market or store, or fresh off a boat as it comes to shore. Check fish and seafood for freshness: a fresh and mild smell, clear eyes, a firm and shiny flesh that is moist (not squishy) and springs back when pressed, and no darkening or drying of the fish's edges.

The soft tissues of a fish easily break down, contaminated by the microbes on their skin, in their guts, and in their gills. The bacteria may be varieties of *Pseudomonas*, or *Salmonella* and *Escherichia coli*. Around the world, people wash fish thoroughly after removing internal organs and gills. Small fish such as sardines are sometimes eaten whole after cooking. After washing and cooking, fish must be kept hot or cold so that bacteria will not multiply and cause illness.

It's worth preparing fish carefully because they're very nutritious. "Fish is fantastic food. For taste and for health, it's pretty

IN THE NETWORK

Some tips for buying fresh fish include checking for clear, bright eyes and shiny flesh, and a smell that is similar to clean water or a bit salty like the sea. The fish gills should be a bright red color, not faded or dark brown.

much unbeatable," said Hugh Fearnley-Whittingstall. "But we can't just take it for granted. It's a precious resource that needs to be consumed thoughtfully. We reckon it helps to know as much as possible about a fish before you buy it—that it's been caught sustainably and handled with respect."

NUTRITION IN FISH

In 2011, *Time* magazine reported that the U.S. government increased the recommended weekly consumption of seafood to 8 ounces (224 grams) or more. Pregnant women were recommended to eat 12 ounces [336 g]. There is a lot of high-quality protein in a serving of fish. Omega-3 polyunsaturated fatty acids in fish oil protect against heart disease and other human health

FISH
FROM THE CATCH TO YOUR TABLE

Fish has been called "health food" and "brain food." Medical studies show how eating fish can be a more healthy choice than eating a lot of processed food products.

Fish that save lives

Researchers are continuing to find evidence that eating saltwater fish regularly cuts your risk of heart disease and stroke.

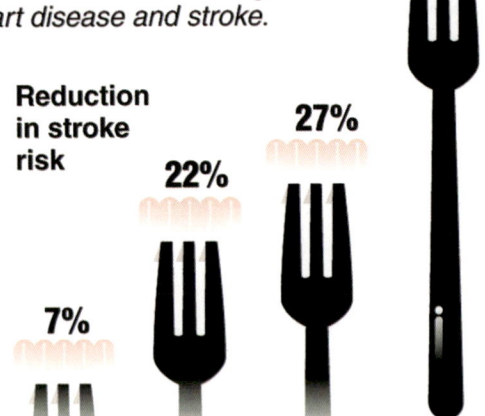

How much fish?
A 14-year study of 80,000 female nurses found a "dose-response" effect – the more fish the nurses ate, the greater the benefit they got

Reduction in stroke risk

- 7% — 1 to 3 times a month
- 22% — 1 time a week
- 27% — 2 to 4 times a week
- 52% — 5 or more times a week

Why fish helps

The protective effect of eating fish is believed to come from the omega-3 fatty acids fish contain

Grams of omega-3 fatty acids per serving (100g or 3.5 oz.)

Fish	Grams
Sardines in oil	3.3
Atlantic mackerel*	2.5
Atlantic salmon	1.2
Striped bass	0.8
Tuna	0.5
Atlantic cod	0.3
Dungeness crab	0.3
Shrimp	0.3
Red snapper	0.2
Swordfish*	0.2
Sole	0.1

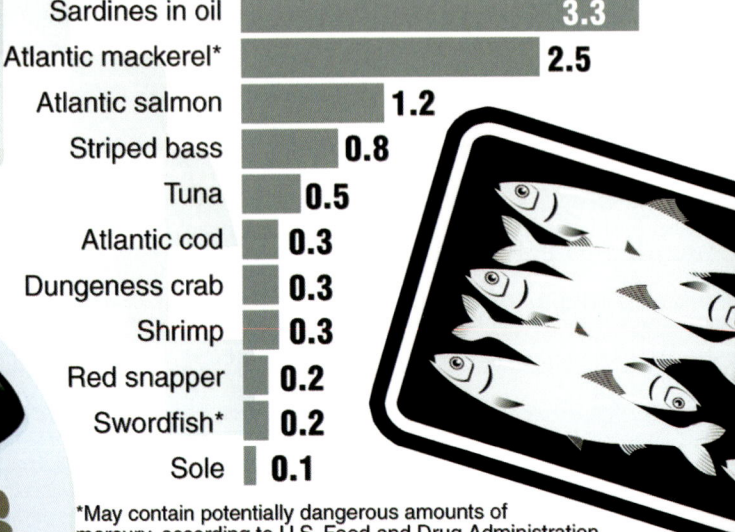

*May contain potentially dangerous amounts of mercury, according to U.S. Food and Drug Administration

Graphic: Paul Trap

IN THE NETWORK

problems. Other fatty acids in fish oil, such as omega-6 and omega-9, are good for nerve and brain health.

The oils in fish contain fat-soluble vitamins such as A, D, E, K, and several kinds of B vitamins. Fish oil is sometimes prescribed to regulate cholesterol in the blood of patients with high blood pressure. Cod liver oil is a particularly good source of vitamins A and D. Fish and fish oils have been linked to improvement of depression disorders.

Minerals in seafood promote good health. There's calcium and phosphorus for growing strong bones, and magnesium and iron for blood cells. Without eating the seafood that contains iodine, people can suffer more from goiter and thyroid problems, weight gain, depression, and memory problems. The World Health Organization reported in 2007 that nearly two billion people didn't get enough iodine in their diet. "Iodine deficiency [is] the single greatest preventable cause of mental retardation," reported the *Lancet* magazine.

Fish support the ecology of rivers and lakes. Migrating fish like salmon leave oceans and return to rivers where they were spawned. In their flesh, they bring nutrients far inland from the ocean. Their flesh is eaten by predators and scavengers, then scattered. It fertilizes forests near streams.

LIFE-THREATENING ALLERGIES

Some food allergies make people get stomachaches or itchy hives. An allergy to shellfish or fish can make a person die. One drop of fishy juices can make an allergic person's throat swell shut. Marion

FISH
FROM THE CATCH TO YOUR TABLE

Science Matters

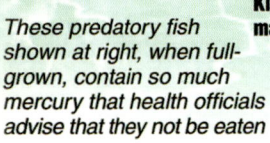
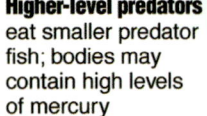
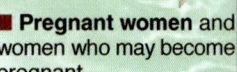

These predatory fish shown at right, when full-grown, contain so much mercury that health officials advise that they not be eaten

- King mackerel
- Swordfish
- Scalloped hammerhead shark
- Tilefish

How fish become toxic

Some saltwater and freshwater fish are contaminated with mercury, a toxic heavy metal, because of what they eat.

What is a food chain?

Each plant and animal species in a natural community eats some species and is eaten by others

Biologists call this web of relationships a food chain

Scavengers eat dead fish, develop high mercury levels

- Black bass
- Sunfish
- Crayfish
- Minnows

Higher-level predators eat smaller predator fish; bodies may contain high levels of mercury

Lower-level predators eat fish, other animals; mercury collects in their bodies

Plant-eaters bring mercury into food chain; contain low amounts of mercury

Lifespan matters: Predators and scavengers that live for several years have longer time to concentrate mercury than fish that die relatively young

People most at risk

- Pregnant women and women who may become pregnant
- Nursing mothers
- Children up to age 10

Mercury can seriously damage the fast-growing brain and nervous system of a child or fetus

Safer food choices

More than once a week: Salmon, shrimp, farm-raised catfish and rainbow trout, flounder, sole, perch, tilapia, clams, scallops

No more than once a week: Tuna (canned), crab, cod, mahi-mahi, haddock, whitefish, herring

Path of mercury pollution

1. Coal- and oil-burning power plants and waste incinerators send mercury into air
2. Water bacteria turn mercury into toxic methyl mercury
3. Small aquatic plants and animals store methyl mercury
4. Toxin gradually works its way up food chain to larger fish, which humans eat

© 2003 KRT

Source: U.S. Food and Drug Admin., U.S. Environmental Protection Agency, Florida Sportsman, Florida Fish & Wildlife Conservation Commission, KRT Illustration Bank
Graphic: Cindy Jones-Hulfachor, Sun Sentinel

Each tiny speck of pollution from a power plant is small. But the heavy metals don't just disappear when the pollution enters water and the food chain. As this poster shows, large fish at the top of the food chain are more likely to contain higher levels of mercury.

IN THE NETWORK

Nestle wrote that twice as many Americans have seafood allergies as have peanut allergies.

Because seafood allergies are so sensitive, the FDA regulates that processed food containing seafood must be labeled very carefully. Ingredient labels must tell whether any kind of fish or shellfish is in the food.

A Fishy Question

What's in a tuna salad sandwich—mayonnaise, pepper, perhaps diced onion, or a little mercury? Nutrition expert Nestle warns that food safety systems must protect people from biohazards "posed by old and new technologies such as mercury in fish from coal-burning power plants."

Activist Sharon Smith admired another activist who pitched a story on ocean pollution by asking, "Have you ever had a mercury sandwich?" This was an opportunity to explain the problem of pollution making its way into fish—and ultimately into people's bodies. Many industrial chemicals and heavy metals do not break down but gradually build up in the food chain, from water-borne phytoplankton to fish, birds, and humans. Even compounds like DDT (which was once used as an insecticide), outlawed for decades, are still being found in wild and farmed fish.

Fishers and cannery workers are careful to wash their cut hands clean of fish slime. In lakes contaminated with giardia or cryptosporidium, a fisher can get sick by touching the water or fish and then his or her face. Bacteria that cause disease are much more common in polluted water.

FISH
FROM THE CATCH TO YOUR TABLE

10 GREAT QUESTIONS TO ASK A NUTRITIONIST

1. Where can I get sustainable seafood locally, with certified labels from the government and industry?
2. What are the food safety rules for preparing and serving seafood safely?
3. What seafood do you recommend to eat if I want to be an athlete?
4. How could eating seafood affect me if I become pregnant?
5. What can you tell me about this brand of canned fish?
6. Is there any kind of seafood that I should not eat?
7. Is it safe to eat this fish that my friend and I caught locally?
8. Do you have any recipes that use fish or shellfish?
9. Is there a local cooking club or classes where I can learn how to cook seafood?
10. Where can I learn about cultural food rules for seafood so that I can serve kosher or halal food?

CHAPTER 5

Making the Rules Count

There are many ways to be advocates for sustainable fishing. The founding of Greenpeace led to the beginning of the end of industrial whale and marine mammal harvesting. Many citizen activist groups have emerged, each with its own goals. A few whales are still killed for markets in Japan and by Inuit for traditional cultural use.

Fish habitat can be improved, and with it, the safety of the food supply. Activist Andy Maser, who kayaks in Washington State, advocates removing dams that block migrating salmon. The removal of several dams near Port Angeles, Washington, is restoring habitat.

Small projects are a practical place to start. One student at the University of Delaware in Newark improved a trout stream when he ripped up an old storm drain. He built a rain garden to filter rainwater draining from a parking lot.

Public Pressure on the Fish Industry

Public outrage over dolphins that drowned in nets caused tuna canning businesses to change to long-line fishing methods instead. All canned tuna now carries "dolphin-friendly" labels to show that

35

FISH
FROM THE CATCH TO YOUR TABLE

Gradual removal of this old dam in Washington State restored the river for spawning salmon.

no dolphins were killed when the tuna was caught. The success of that letter campaign and boycott by consumers and activists inspires many people.

Other activism choices that bring issues to the forefront include political campaigning; poster making; and peaceful assemblies such as marches, sit-ins, and teach-ins. Boycotts and carrotmobs can make consumer purchases powerful. Fisher calls consumer boycotts "the only meaningful action that can be taken." When people participate in passing laws to protect their food supply and environment, they feel empowered to insist that industry comply with the laws.

As consumers, young people can ask the servers at restaurants or the fish retailer which fish is in season before making a decision about what fish to purchase. Ask, too, about where and how the seafood was caught. When businesses realize that customers are interested in their products, they are more aware of the sustainability and quality of their fish. Wise consumers should not purchase fresh fish if the employees working with the products are not wearing clean clothing, hair coverings, or throwaway gloves.

MAKING THE RULES COUNT

GMO Food or Frankenfood?

Changes done to genetically modified organisms (GMOs) such as fish have many effects. Some effects are not obvious until living fish are out of the laboratory. "By 2001, Maryland was the only state to ban a genetically modified food, in this case fish in waterways that connect to other bodies of water," wrote Nestle. "Consumer groups, chefs, and some scientists have filed lawsuits and organized petition campaigns to compel the FDA to institute labeling and safety testing."

A/F Protein Inc., an American company, has genetically engineered (GE) Atlantic salmon with the genes for a growth hormone from Chinook salmon that was inserted into their eggs, reported Greenpeace. GE salmon grow four times faster than normal, and some have deformed heads. If these salmon escape from a fish farm, it could adversely affect the wild salmon population. In 2011, the FDA was under pressure from AquaBounty, based in Massachusetts, to approve GMO salmon. Some fish farms refuse to raise transgenic salmon (salmon that have had their genetic material altered). Consumers can write to grocery stores and distributors about their refusal to eat GE or GMO salmon.

Resource Management

The West Hawaii Fisheries Council was formed in 1998 to advise the state of Hawaii on creating new rules to manage fisheries

FISH
FROM THE CATCH TO YOUR TABLE

resources. On the council's advice, at least 30 percent of the west coast of Hawaii is designated as fish replenishment areas. "Even now," observed Regina Gregory on the EcoTipping Points Web site, "small areas of the Hawaiian islands managed under traditional practices show as much fish stock as the formal marine life conservation districts, where no fishing is allowed at all."

Class Projects

Students can get involved in local and national projects for fishing sustainability. Some of the successful national projects and programs include the following:

- Students in a Hawaii beach-cleaning project wrote a resolution that their county council passed in 2007, banning smoking on Kahalu'u Bay Beach.
- The Federation of Student Anglers operates fishing programs in middle schools, high schools, and colleges throughout the United States and has a scholarship program.
- In Montana's Fish, Wildlife, and Parks Department, a high school student was selected to sit on the Fisheries Review panel.
- The City University of New York (CUNY) found an internship for a high school senior in a biology lab, where the student learned to dissect fish.
- A competition for high school students, called the National Ocean Science Bowl, is sponsored by the Consortium for Ocean leadership and the National Marine Educators Association. It tests students' knowledge of the marine sciences.

MAKING THE RULES COUNT

Besides these, there are many opportunities for teens who want to learn more about fish and their habitats.

Garbage

The easiest pollution to clean up is garbage. Even far out at sea, garbage chokes fish and sea birds that mistake trash for food. Gray whales are at risk because they feed by taking large mouthfuls of the ocean bottom and filter out small sea animals to swallow. Other protected sea animals that people once ate, such as seals and turtles, are also at risk.

On Earth Day, April 25, 2011, Project Aware organized more than 230 scuba-diving events. Volunteer divers cleared garbage and debris from dive locations around the world. "Our best solution is to prevent trash from entering the system," said marine mammal researcher Rob Williams.

The Project AWARE Web page (www.projectaware.org) contains information about programs to restore ecosystems and fish habitat. People can get involved through their work or schools or sports interests.

FISH
FROM THE CATCH TO YOUR TABLE

Legislation

It's hard to enforce fishing quotas. "The United Nations agreement on the Law of the Sea states that outside of offshore boundaries, no one owns the ocean," wrote science columnist Bob McDonald. National governments try to manage nearby seafood resources. After the British Petroleum oil spill in the Gulf of Mexico in 2010, there is ongoing concern about safe seafood harvesting. The FDA and the National Oceanic and Atmospheric Administration (NOAA) teamed up with state agencies and the National Marine Fisheries Service and the U.S. Environmental Protection Agency to try to recover valuable seafood resources.

In 2009, President Barack Obama set up an Interagency Ocean Policy Task Force, promoting conservation of the ocean, coasts, and the Great Lakes. The task force's recommendations established a national policy for water resource stewardship. Furthermore, the Obama administration's national Clean Water Framework on April 27, 2011, "recognizes the importance of clean water and healthy watersheds to our economy, environment, and communities."

"Many countries have realized that environmental conservation is good for the economy—and they're taking action," wrote the Coastal Alliance for Aquaculture Reform, an organization based in Vancouver, British Columbia. Around the world, there are many water management and seafood resource management boards. Seafood resource management functions best where local interests are represented. "Everyone can do something about food," declared Nestle. "The food revolution has arrived."

GLOSSARY

advocate A person who publicly supports or champions a cause or policy; to publicly recommend or support something.

benthic Relating to the organisms living in deep water.

biohazard A human health risk caused by infection.

calories How much energy a person's body gets from food. Carbohydrates and proteins have 4.5 calories per gram; fat has 9 calories per gram.

carrotmob The opposite of a boycott. Consumers buy goods or services from a business, prearranged with the use of social media. The idiom refers to driving a donkey by offering it a carrot.

cartilaginous Made of cartilage; having a skeleton of cartilage.

cliché A phrase or opinion that is overused.

comply To meet specific standards or rules.

contaminate To make something impure, or to poison or pollute.

cryptosporidium A microorganism that lives in lakes and rivers and can make people ill.

ecosystem A biological community of interacting organisms and their physical environment.

Escherichia coli A bacterium that lives in human and animal intestines. Some varieties cause mild or severe illness.

fatty omega acids Oily fats in fish and other foods; essential nutrition for good function and growth of nerves and brain cells.

fermenting Food processing that introduces a microorganism, such as a bacterium like the one that ferments milk into yogurt, into food.

giardia A microorganism that lives in lakes and rivers and can make people ill.

FISH
FROM THE CATCH TO YOUR TABLE

goiter A swollen neck, caused by an enlarged thyroid gland.

halal Food that is permitted under Islamic law.

heavy metal Metals such as lead, that accumulate as a poison in the bodies of water life and in the food chain.

kosher Food that is permitted by Jewish law.

marine conservationist A scientist who works to protect and preserve the biological community of the seas and oceans.

mercury A heavy metal released in the smoke from coal-burning power plants and pulp mills.

neurological Dealing with the nerves and nervous system.

pasteurize To treat fish through a heat process, usually after the product is already sealed in a container or package.

phytoplankton A microscopic organism of the sea or freshwater that consists of tiny plants.

replenishment The return or rebuilding of a stock or supply to a former level or condition.

Salmonella A bacterium, common in seafood, that can grow in food at room temperature. It causes vomiting and diarrhea.

sonar A system to detect objects underwater by using sound pulses. The pulses are measured when they return after being reflected.

sustainable Able to use a resource in ways that support the local economy and maintain the local environment.

vitamin A complex molecule present in many kinds of fresh food and fish oils, essential for good health.

FOR MORE INFORMATION

Canadian Council of Food and Nutrition
2810 Matheson Boulevard East, 1st Floor
Mississauga, ON L4W 4X7
Canada
(905) 625-5746
Web site: http://www.nin.ca
Health professionals in this Canadian organization teach nutrition and food issues to the public.

Center for Food Safety
660 Pennsylvania Avenue SE, #302
Washington, DC 20003
(202) 547-9359
Web site: http://www.centerforfoodsafety.org
This nonprofit group works toward stopping harmful food production, including in aquaculture, and promotes sustainable alternatives.

Center for Science in the Public Interest (CSPI)
1220 L Street NW
Washington, DC 20005
(202) 332-9110
Web site: http://www.cspinet.org
The CSPI is a nonprofit, health-advocacy organization supported by subscribers to its *Nutrition Action Healthletter*, with no industry or government funding. It led efforts to pass the law requiring nutrition labeling, and it has publicized the nutritional content of many popular restaurant foods.

ChooseMyPlate.gov
USDA Center for Nutrition Policy and Promotion
3101 Park Center Drive, Room 1034
Alexandria, VA 22302-1594
(888) 779-7264
Web site: http://www.choosemyplate.gov
The U.S. Department of Agriculture Web site www.choosemyplate.gov (formerly MyPyramid.gov) lets visitors set up a personal eating plan and track activity and eating levels, with recommendations for healthy kinds and amounts of food.

FoodSafety.gov
U.S. Department of Health and Human Services
Web Communications and New Media Division
200 Independence Avenue SW

FISH
FROM THE CATCH TO YOUR TABLE

Washington, DC 20201

Web site: http://www
.foodsafety.gov

This Web site is the gateway to information about food safety in the United States. It provides information about food recalls and alerts, including those involving seafood.

Slow Food USA

20 Jay Street, #313

Brooklyn, NY 11201

(718) 260-8000

Web site: http://www
.slowfoodusa.org

The Slow Food movement has many informal chapters in countries around the world, encouraging people to eat mindfully, enjoying local and seasonal food.

U.S. Department of Agriculture (USDA)

1400 Independence Avenue SW

Washington, DC 20250

(202) 720-2791

Web site: http://www.usda.gov

The USDA publishes information on all aspects of agriculture, including food, nutrition, research, and science. Its Natural Resources Conservation Service helps with fish and wildlife management.

U.S. Fish and Wildlife Service (USFWS)

Division of Information Resources and Technology Management

4401 North Fairfax Drive

Suite 340

Arlington, VA 22203

(800) 344-9453

Web site: http://www.fws.gov

The USFWS works to conserve, protect, and enhance fish, wildlife, plants, and their habitats for the benefit of everyone in the United States.

Web Sites

Due to the changing nature of Internet links, Rosen Publishing has developed an online list of Web sites related to the subject of this book. This site is updated regularly. Please use this link to access the list:

http://www.rosenlinks.com/food/fish

FOR FURTHER READING

Coté, Charlotte. Spirits of Our Whaling Ancestors: Revitalizing Makah and Nuu-chah-nulth Traditions. Vancouver, BC, Canada: UBC Press, 2010.

Giddens, Sandra. Making Smart Choices About Food, Nutrition, and Lifestyles (Making Smart Choices). New York, NY: Rosen Publishing Group, 2008.

Harmon, Daniel E. Fish, Meat, and Poultry: Dangers in the Food Supply (What's in Your Food? Recipe for Disaster). New York, NY: Rosen Publishing Group, 2008.

Jensen, Derrick, and Stephanie McMillan. As the World Burns: 50 Simple Things You Can Do to Stay in Denial. New York, NY: Seven Stories Press, 2007.

Johanson, Paula. Fried, Fast, and Processed: The Incredibly Disgusting Story. New York, NY: Rosen Publishing Group, 2011.

Johanson, Paula. Processed Food (What's in Your Food? Recipe for Disaster). New York, NY: Rosen Publishing Group, 2008.

Pollan, Michael. Food Rules: An Eater's Manual. New York, NY: Penguin, 2010.

Pollan, Michael. The Omnivore's Dilemma for Kids: The Secrets Behind What You Eat. New York, NY: Dial Books Young Readers, 2009.

Smith, Alisa, and J. B. MacKinnon. The 100-Mile Diet: A Year of Local Eating. Toronto, ON, Canada: Random House, 2007.

Smith, Sharon J. The Young Activist's Guide to Building a Green Movement & Changing the World. Berkeley, CA: Earth Island Institute, 2011.

BIBLIOGRAPHY

Centers for Disease Control and Prevention. "Workplace Safety & Health Topics—Commercial Fishing Safety." July 11, 2011. Retrieved October 4, 2011 (http://www.cdc.gov/niosh/topics/fishing).

Fearnley-Whittingstall, Hugh, and Nick Fisher. *The River Cottage Fish Book*. London, England: Bloomsbury, 2007.

Greenpeace. "Artificial Organisms." Greenpeace Genetic Engineering Archive. Retrieved September 5, 2011 (http://archive.greenpeace.org/geneng/highlights/gmo/GEfishafp.htm).

Gregory, Regina. "USA-Hawaii (Big Island)-The West Hawai'i Fisheries Council: A Forum for Coral Reef Stakeholders." *EcoTipping Points Project*. Retrieved September 24, 2011 (http://www.ecotippingpoints.com/our-stories/indepth/usa-hawaii-fisheries-council-community-participation.html).

Gronewold, Nathanial, and ClimateWire. "Pollution and Climate Change Accelerate Ocean Degradation." *Scientific American*, June 22, 2011. Retrieved June 24, 2011 (http://www.scientificamerican.com/article.cfm?id=pollution-climate-change-accelerate-ocean-degradation).

Houpt, Simon. "Thirty-second Spots." *Globe and Mail*, June 3, 2011, p. B6.

"Iodine Deficiency—Way to Go Yet." *Lancet*, July 12, 2008, Vol. 372, No. 9,642, p. 88.

Jenkins, McKay. *What's Gotten into Us? Staying Healthy in a Toxic World*. New York, NY: Random House, 2011.

McDonald, Bob. "We Can't Continue to Ignore the Failing Health of Our Oceans." CBC News, June 23, 2011. Retrieved July 20, 2011 (http://www.cbc.ca/news/technology/quirks-quarks-blog/2011/06/oceans-zero.html).

"Mystery Fish." *Consumer Reports*, December 2011, pp. 18–22.

Nestle, Marion. *Safe Food: The Politics of Food Safety*. 2nd ed. Berkeley, CA: University of California Press, 2010.

Pauly, Daniel. *5 Easy Pieces: How Fishing Impacts Marine Ecosystems*. Washington, DC: Island Press, 2010.

Rosenthal, Elisabeth. "Tests Reveal Mislabeling of Fish." *New York Times*, May 26, 2011. Retrieved May 31, 2011 (http://www.nytimes.com/2011/05/27/science/earth/27fish.html).

Stengel, Richard. "Aquaculture and the Future of Food." *Time*, July 18, 2011, Vol. 178, No. 3.

Wallace, Scott, and Brian Gisborne. "Preface." *Basking Sharks: The Slaughter of BC's Gentle Giants*. Vancouver, BC, Canada: Transmontanus/New Star Books, 2006, p. 12.

Walsh, Brian. "Seafood's Next Wave." *Time*, July 18, 2011, Vol. 178, No. 3.

INDEX

A
allergy to fish and shellfish, 31–33

B
bacteria and fish, 20, 28, 33
bycatch, 12, 13

C
canning, 15
cod, overfishing of, 5–6, 27
conservation, 40

D
dried fish, 15–16

E
environmental damage done by fishing, 6, 10–11, 21, 40

F
fish as renewable resource, 26–27
fish eggs, 16
fish farming, 11–12, 37
fishing, history of, 4–6, 7–9
fish oil, 29–31
fish products, 19–20
food safety, 13, 28, 36, 40
freshness, and buying fish, 28–29
frozen fish, 16–17

G
genetically modified fish, 37

H
herring, overfishing of, 27

I
importation of seafood, 22
irradiation of seafood, 18–19, 20

L
labels, food, 25–26, 33
legislation for fishing, 40
local food, eating, 22–24

N
nutrition and fish, 29–30, 34

O
offal, 13–14
overfishing, 5–6, 21, 26–27

P
packaging of fish, 24–25
paralytic shellfish poisoning, 20
pollution, effect on fish of, 33, 39
preparation/processing of fish, 13–21
    and food safety, 13, 28
preservation methods, 14

S
shellfish harvesting, 12, 20
smoked fish, 17
sustainable fishing, 35–40

T
transportation of fish, 22–27

V
vacuum packing, 17–18, 24
Vibrio bacteria contamination, 20

FISH
FROM THE CATCH TO YOUR TABLE

About the Author

For more than twenty years, Paula Johanson has worked as a writer, teacher, and editor. For a salmon enhancement program, she waded up Goldstream River feeding coho salmon fry every weekend for four years. She operated an organic-method market garden for fifteen years, selling produce and wool at farmers' markets. As an outdoor enthusiast, Johanson enjoyed touring docks, fish packers and canneries, clam gardens, and fish farms for this book. Her nonfiction books on science, health, and literature include Jobs in Sustainable Agriculture, Processed Food, and Fake Foods: Fried, Fast, and Processed.

Photo Credits

Cover, pp. 1, 7, 13, 22, 28, 35 (salmon fillet) © istockphoto.com/ffolas: cover, p. 1 (rainbow trout) © istockphoto.com/Irina Kozhemyakina; cover. p. 1 (water) © istockphoto.com/Jens Carsten Rosemann; cover, pp. 1, 21 (tablecloth) © istockphoto.com/milanfoto; p. 3 (background texture) © istockphoto.com/P Wei; pp. 4–5 © AP Images; p. 8 O. Louis Mazzatenta/National Geographic/Getty Images; p. 10 Alaska Stock Images/National Geographic Stock; p. 14 Ingram Publishing/Thinkstock; p. 15 © AP Images; p. 16 Shutterstock/chiracbogdan; p. 18 Martin Hospach/Getty Images; p. 19 istockphoto/Thinkstock; p. 21 (cutting board) © istockphoto.com/mark wragg; p. 23 Massachusetts Office of Travel & Tourism; p. 25 © Ambient Images, Inc./SuperStock; p. 26 Karen Huang; p. 29 Shutterstock/Elena Rostunova; p. 30 Trap/MCT/Newscom; p. 32 Jones-Huffachor KRT/Newscom; p. 34 (vitruvian man) © istockphoto.com/Max Delson Martins Santos, (measuring tape) © istockphoto.com/Zoran Kolundzija; p. 36 Courtesy of PacifiCorp; p. 39 Project AWARE; cover and interior background images © istockphoto/Chan Yee Kee (metal surface), © istockphoto.com/Laura Stanley (chain).

Designer: Michael Moy; Editor: Kathy Kuhtz Campbell;
Photo Researcher: Marty Levick